D0598381

DISCARD

SAN JUAN ISLAND LIBRARY
1010 GUARD STREET
FRIDAY HARBOR, WA 98250

2/02

Homework Busters

Bill Thompson

Illustrated by Debi Ani

Library of Congress Cataloging-in-Publication Data Available

10 9 8 7 6 5 4 3 2 1

First published in the UK in 2000 by Big Fish. Distributed by Sterling Publishing Company, Inc. 387, Park Avenue South, New York, N.Y. 100016.

Distributed in Canada by Sterling Publishing, c/o Canadian Manda Group, One Atlantic Avenue, Suite 105, Toronto, Ontario, Canada M6K 3E7.

Copyright © Big Fish 2000

All rights reserved.

ISBN 0-8069-3675-4

Printed in China

Project management: Honor Head
Editor: Anna Claybourne
Designer: Angela Ashton
Illustrator: Debi Ani
Menu bar icons: Chris Swee

Screen shots of Microsoft ® Internet Explorer on pages 18 and 45 used by permission from Microsoft Corporation.

Screen shot of shuttle space suit site on page 18 used by permission of NASA.

Every effort has been made to contact the copyright holders of the material reproduced in this book.

CONTENTS

Welcome to Homework Busters

Welcome to **Homework Busters** – a book that shows you how to use the Internet to help with homework. This section explains exactly what the Internet can do.

Why use the Net?

The Internet is a cool place to visit. You can have a great time finding things to do, games to play and people to talk to. The Net is also very useful for looking things up and finding things out. That's why it's so handy when you've got a pile of homework to do.

On the Net, you can find facts, practice skills, and get help and advice from real people or from on-line 'robots'. You can also find pictures, sounds, and even video clips to add to your work. You can even hand in your homework by e-mail, or put it on a website.

Seen it all before?

You may have been on the Internet before. Maybe you use it at school to look things up. You might have an e-mail penfriend, or perhaps you've even built your own website. But whether you're a webwiz or a complete beginner, this book can help you get on-line and get more from the Net.

I'm stuck... I wish I could write like Shakespeare!

I need to learn the 15 X table!

Help! I need a picture of a mongoose!

When did the first spacecraft land on the moon?

Here's what we'll do

We can't do your homework for you – getting someone else to do all the work isn't the idea anyway. But just because you've got to work doesn't mean you can't have fun.

- We'll look at how to find the stuff you want, and how to use cool search engines, directories, and indexes to get there fast.

- We'll show you different ways to keep in touch on-line, and explain how you can use chat, e-mail, and newsgroups to help with homework.

- We'll look at the programs you can get from the Internet to help you memorize things and keep you organized. That way you can get your homework done and still have time to enjoy yourself!

- We'll show you how to make your finished work look good, on screen and in print.

Let's get started!

Each page in this book will work on its own, so you don't have to start at page one and keep on reading. And there are lots of places where you'll want to link up to the Net to explore before you carry on reading. That's fine – you'll learn a lot more that way than by just sitting here reading. So let's get homework-busting!

Look out for boxes like this...

Quicklinks
These 'quicklinks' boxes tell you about useful places on the Net, that you can get to through the **Internet @ction** website. Go to http://www. internetaction.net.

You're on a mission to uncharted space. Not the normal space you live in, but cyberspace, the space behind your computer screen. Cyberspace is a word for all the information and programs on all the computers connected to the Internet.

What is the Internet?

The Internet, or Net for short, is a network of computers all around the world. The Net links them together so that they can share information – all 60 million of them, from the smallest PC to the biggest mainframe.

What's it for?

People use the Net for all sorts of things:

- Sending 'electronic mail' or e-mail.
- Chatting to each other over long distances.
- Sharing information on the World Wide Web.

But what does it all mean?

The Web

The Web is a way to store information on a computer so that everyone on the Internet can see it on their computer screen. It's a great place to find out facts. A screenful of information on the Web is called a web page. A website is a collection of web pages that go together.

E-mail

E-mail, short for electronic mail, is the way people use the Internet to send messages to each other. When you send an e-mail message, it travels down the phone line or cable, across the Internet, and into the other person's computer for them to pick up. It's not just words – you can e-mail pictures, sounds, video clips, or even whole programs!

Chat

Using chat services, you can 'talk' to another Internet user while you're both on-line, by typing messages which they can see straight away. It's a great way to stay in touch.

What you need

Before you can use any of the great things on the Internet you need to get connected – or 'go on-line'. You can use almost any sort of computer on the Internet, although PCs running Windows® and Apple Macintosh computers are used most often.

Most people connect to the Internet from home using a special box called a modem. You plug one end into your computer and the other end into a phone socket. The modem translates computer data into sounds which can be sent over the phone line.

Better ask whoever pays the phone bill before you link up to the Net!

Where do I get the software?

You'll need a web browser, and programs to do e-mail and chat, if you want to get the most out of the Internet.

Your ISP (see below) will send you a CD or disk with a web browser and an e-mail program on it. You install them when you set up your Internet connection. You can also get CDs free with computer magazines and in some supermarkets and stores.

You can find chat programs – and lots of other stuff – for free on the Internet itself. The **Internet @ction** website will point you in the right direction.

Get an ISP

You also need an Internet Service Provider or ISP. ISPs are companies that link your computer to their big on-line computers. They pass information between your computer and the rest of the Net. Some ISPs charge a fee, and some are free. Of course, you may also have to pay for the phone calls you make each time you want to get connected.

Finding stuff

So you're on-line and looking for the facts you need to do your homework. Where are you going to start? First of all, you need to know how websites work.

Overload!

The World Wide Web is big. Really big. It has over a billion different files – or 'pages' – and thousands more get added each day. If the Web was a book, it would be over a mile thick, and the contents page would fill a library on its own! Even if you had a table strong enough to put it on, you'd never find what you wanted. But the Web is much easier to use than an enormous book. It has ways of helping you find things, which are explained on the next few pages.

What is a website?

A website is a collection of web pages, usually on the same subject or written by the same people. Each page can have words, photographs, pictures, sounds, and even programs. Web pages are stored on computers called servers. When you ask to see a web page, it is sent to your computer in code form. Your browser (part of your Internet software) translates the code into the page you see on the screen.

> Some web pages are too long to see all at once. You have to scroll up and down to read them.

What's in a name?

Each web page has its own special name, or URL – short for Uniform Resource Locator. A URL looks like this:

This is the part of the server where the page is stored.

http://www.internetaction.co.uk/hb/index.html

This part shows that this is a web page.

This is the name of the server computer the website is on.

This is the filename of the web page itself.

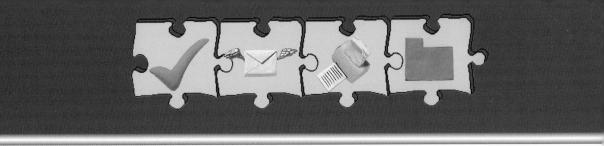

Finding the right place

Every page on every website has its own URL. All you have to do is type the URL into your browser screen, and it will take you straight to the right page. How do you know which sites to visit? Well, you might see a URL in a magazine or on TV. Or your teacher may give you a URL to try. Perhaps a friend will e-mail you the URL of a website you should visit – just copy the address into your browser. Sometimes, just clicking on a URL in an e-mail launches your browser and takes you to the site.

Moving around

Once you've got to a web page and had a look at it, you'll want to explore. You can do this by clicking on a link – a way to jump from one page to another. A link could be a word, a picture or an icon. Here's how to spot one:

Planet

Words that link to other pages are usually in blue and underlined. They are called hypertext links.

click here

Some links look like buttons or switches, with 'click here' written next to them or on them.

Some links are small pictures, or icons. For example, an envelope symbol might link to a page showing e-mail addresses.

Link

If you see the pointer change from an arrow to a hand, you know you're over a link. Click on it to see where it goes.

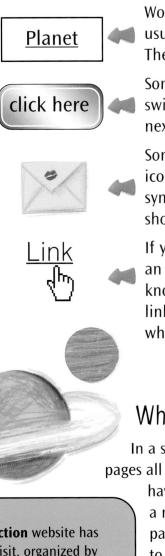

Where do links go?

In a single website, there may be several pages all joined together by links. Most sites have a main page or 'home page', with a menu – a list of links to the other pages on the site. Links can also go to completely different websites. For example, a site about outer space might have links to other good space sites, so you can get to them easily.

Quicklinks
The **Internet @ction** website has lists of useful places to visit, organized by subject. To go to the **Internet @ction** site, type http://www.internetaction.net into your browser.

Searching

If you're given a URL to start with, it's easy to find the right page. But what if you don't even know where to begin? If you want the answer to a specific question, you'll need to search the Web.

Searching in a website

If you've already found a website that might contain the right info, the fastest way to get where you want is to search the site. Many big websites have a search option. Just type in what you want to find out about, and the search program looks through all the pages on the website to see if it's there.

Looking around

But what if you don't even know which website you want? What you really need is a way to search through all the pages on the whole of the Web. The solution is a spider. A spider is a program that crawls all over the Web, following every link it can find and keeping track of the contents of web pages in a special database. Using a program called a search engine, you can then search through the database to find out which web pages have the information you need.

Search engines

There are lots of different search engines. None of them has details of the whole Web – it's too big and changing too fast for them to keep up. But a search engine is the best way so far invented of finding stuff on the Web.

How to search

When you go to a search engine or a directory, you'll see an empty search box. This is where you type in words, called 'keywords', to do with the thing you're looking for. Then you click on the 'Search', 'Go', or 'Find' button. A few seconds later, you'll get a list of results, or 'hits'. On a search engine, these will probably be individual web pages. On a directory, they will be websites. The list will tell you a bit about each site or page so that you can decide whether to look at it. It will also have a link to each page, so you can just point and click to go there.

Search the Web for:

voyager|

Go!

Directories

As well as search engines, the Web has lots of directories. A directory is a list of other websites, organized a bit like the index of a book. When you want to find a website about space, or Egypt, or electricity, you can look through the directory's list, or search it, until you find a link to the sort of site you need.

What to type

It's useful to know what kinds of keywords work best in search engines and directories. Let's say you're trying to find out about the Voyager spacecraft. In a search engine, you might type in:

```
voyager spacecraft
```

The search engine will look for any mention of the Voyager spacecraft in the web pages it knows about. In a directory, it would be better to type:

```
space exploration
```

The directory won't look at every single page, but it will find all the websites it knows about which deal with space. You can then pick one of these websites, go to its own search program, and type:

```
voyager
```

to see if it has anything about Voyager.

Don't get stuck in a rut

Not every website is in a directory or search engine, and not all directories and search engines have the same information. So don't rely on just one. It's a good idea to look at two or three each time you have a search to do. And you should try a search engine *and* a directory – that way you're less likely to miss stuff out.

> Most search engines ignore capital letters. Just use small letters for everything.

Quicklinks

We've put together a list of the best directories and search engines to help you find what you need for your homework. They're fast, they're big and they're child-friendly. To get to our list, go to the **Internet @ction** website: http://www.internetaction.net.

Advanced searching

Searching sounds easy. The problem is, it's a bit too easy. You can end up with all sorts of information you don't need. Here's how to do clever searches that will narrow down the results until you get what you're looking for.

Simple searches

Suppose you type:

```
mercury
```

into a search engine. You'll get hundreds of thousands of pages! Some will be about a metal called mercury, some will be about Mercury the Roman god, and some will be about the planet Mercury. Lots of them will be about cars or computers or books, or almost anything that has the word 'mercury' in it. That's because search engines can't reason like a human brain. All they do is go through every page in their database and look to see if it has the seven letters m, e, r, c, u, r, and y in it, in that order.

Piles of pages

If you only want to know about the planet Mercury, you need to act clever. But it's not easy. For example, if you search for:

```
planet mercury
```

you'll get even more pages! That's because most search engines will look for pages with 'planet' and pages with 'mercury' and give you them both. What you really want are pages which have both 'mercury' *and* 'planet'. So what do you do?

Quicklinks
On the **Internet @ction** website are lists of search engines and directories you can use to get some real searching practice on-line.

Getting clever

Luckily, you can narrow down your search, using a few simple rules. This is called advanced searching. Every search engine works in a slightly different way. We'll show you how to do an advanced search on AltaVista, because it's one of the biggest and fastest. If you're using a different search engine, just read its help pages to see how it works. (They're all quite similar.) First, click on 'advanced search'. (In some search engines this has another name, such as 'power search'.)

Then, to find pages which have both the word 'mercury' and the word 'planet' on them, type:

in the box. The '+' tells AltaVista that you're looking for pages with both words on them. And suppose you didn't want to see pages that talked about the metal mercury. Just type:

The '-' tells AltaVista to choose pages that contain the word 'mercury', but not the word 'metal'. Simple!

Boole rules!

Lots of websites will let you do a Boolean search – but you have to know what one is! Boolean searches use a system invented by a 19th-century mathematician called George Boole. Instead of using symbols like '+' and '-', Boole used the words AND, OR, and NOT.

First, click on the button in your search engine marked 'Boolean search'.

Then type in a sentence such as:

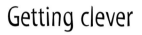

The search engine will look for pages that have the words 'mercury' and 'planet' in them, but not the word 'god'. Once you get good at Boolean searches, you'll be zooming across the Internet like an expert, and finding stuff a lot faster than your friends.

Don't get lost!

Zooming around the Web is loads of fun. You can click on links and head off wherever you want. But when you've got homework, you don't want to lose track of those useful sites.

Backwards and forwards

Web browsers have lots of ways to help you keep track of things. The 'Back' button is the simplest. Every time you visit a web page, your friendly browser keeps a record of its URL. When you click on 'Back' you'll be taken to the last page you were at, then the one before that, and so on. Browsers also have a 'Forward' button so you can retrace your steps as many times as you like.

> On some browsers, the 'Back' and 'Forward' buttons look like arrows.
> ◁ ▷

Mark your way

'Back', 'Forward', and 'History' buttons are useful, but what you really need is a record of the sites you like best, so you can return to them quickly and easily. To do this, browsers have a button called either 'Favorites' or 'Bookmarks'. When you find a site you like, click on this button, and the URL will be stored for you. When you want to find the site again, open up your list and select the right URL using the mouse.

History is fun

If you like, you can even take a look at your browser's record of the pages you've visited recently. If you click on the 'History' button, your browser will show you a long list of URLs – your web-browsing history. Use the mouse to select a URL you'd like to visit again.

> Long URLs take a long time to write down. Luckily I've got a browser to do it for me!

Save me!

Sometimes you'll want to keep copies of things you find on the Web. Then you can look at them again later, when you're not on-line. This is especially useful for homework, when you might want to look at something several times. You can even copy pictures from the Web to illustrate your homework.

To do this, use your browser's 'Save' button to turn a web page or an e-mail message into a file you can store on your computer. After you press 'Save', follow the instructions to create the new file and store it somewhere handy. It's a good idea to create a new folder on your computer for the things you save. Call it something like 'My Internet Stuff'.

Picture tip

When you save a web page, you will also have to save all the pictures separately or they won't be there when you want them. Some browsers only save the HTML (the words) and not the images. We'll talk about HTML later.

Whose work is it?

Remember that the things you find on the Internet don't belong to you! It's usually OK to use photos and illustrations for school work, as long as you don't sell them. When you use something from the Web in your homework, you should always include an acknowledgement – a note saying which website you got it from.

It's easy for anyone to put stuff on the Net. That's good, because it means there's lots to look at on-line. But it also means it's hard to tell whether the things you find are accurate and up-to-date.

Who do you trust?

The first thing to ask yourself is 'Who is saying this?' Look at what you're reading, think about where it's coming from, and then decide whether to believe it or not.

You'll find a lot of content on websites published by...

A TV station

A newspaper

A university

An encyclopedia

A magazine

A government agency, such as NASA

Be skeptical of what you read on-line. People often use their websites to express opinions. Or they might have just made a mistake.

E-mails

Usually you can't be sure things in an e-mail are true. However, if you've e-mailed an expert to ask them a question (see page 22), you can probably rely on their answer.

Newsgroups

Watch out – on a newsgroup (see page 24), it's often hard to tell who knows what they're talking about and who doesn't.

So what do I do?

Websites

Websites are easier to work with because you can tell a lot from the URL. Some sources of information are very reliable.

Double-check!

If you're not sure the facts you're reading are right, don't worry – just double-check. This might mean looking stuff up in a library or newspaper, or even just asking someone (like your teacher). Or you could search the Web for another site on the same subject, to see if the facts match up. If lots of sensible sites say the same thing, it's probably right.

Fuzzy facts

Sometimes, nobody knows the truth! This happens most of all with news. For example, after a big earthquake it can be days or even weeks before we know how many people were killed or injured or lost their homes. Newspapers and TV programs will say things like 'an estimated 100,000 people are homeless', but this is just a good guess. If you look at several news sites, you'll often get several different figures.

What to do

When there are lots of different figures, how do you know which is true? Well, they're all guesses, based on different information. What if you have to do a report on, say, an earthquake for your homework and you want to put how many people were made homeless? You can either choose the number you think is most likely to be accurate, or you can say something like this:

Dusty cobwebs

Don't forget that things change. Sometimes people put up a website but never come back to update it, so it just sits there gathering virtual dust. An old, out-of-date website like this is called a cobweb.

Estimates of the number of people made homeless vary between 50,000 and 150,000. The true figure is still unknown.

A good website will say when it was last updated. Look for this before you rely on the facts you find.

Last updated 03/04/00

Quicklinks

For the latest information on current news stories go to the **Internet @ction** website for a list of sites which will give you up-to-the minute news reviews.

Sample project: Space

Now you know what to do, why not try out your new Net research skills on a real-life project? Your mission: find out about outer space!

Space search

You probably know by now that just typing 'space' into a search engine will give you far too much information. You'll get every site that has the word 'space' in it – from estate agents to dancing schools.

But what you really need is a big site with lots of useful space facts. Don't worry, there are plenty out there! Using a combination of methods, you can make sure you find them.

Here we go...

We're going to show you some real web pages and URLs. Remember that the Net is changing all the time, so if you go to them, they may not be quite the same. But there will probably be even better stuff for you to find when you go searching...

Use a directory

If you search for:

outer space

on the *Yahooligans!* kids' directory, you'll find six places to look, including Outer Orbit: Ask an Astronomer.

Use a search engine

Search engines are good for finding out something very specific. If you type:

space+suit+shuttle

into a search engine, you should be able to find a picture of the space suit worn by shuttle astronauts.

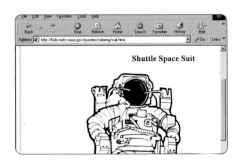

Find a big site

Sometimes you'll find one big website that can provide everything you need. For example, NASA, the American organization for exploring and studying space, has a great website. Some of it is designed especially for kids. All you have to do is follow the links to the most useful pages for your project.

You can find the NASA site easily by doing a search for 'NASA' in any search engine or directory.

Guess the URL

You can sometimes play 'guess the URL' to find a big website.

Just take the organization's name...
NASA

add 'www.' to the beginning...
www.NASA

and try .com or .gov or .net at the end...
www.NASA.gov

Quicklinks

To make things even easier, on the **Internet @ction** website we've included links to a useful selection of space sites – including NASA. Go to: http://www.internetaction.net.

Gathering information

As you browse, copy useful bits of text, pictures, and facts to use later. If you've got a printer, you can also print out web pages to read later or keep as reference. When you see a page you like, just click on the 'Print' button in your browser. Once you've got the facts you need, you can put your project together. For help with this, see page 30.

Multimedia search

If you can't find what you need on the Net, don't forget there are other places to look things up...

- A big encyclopedia might have the facts you need.

- Look in a library or bookstore for books about space.

- There might be a CD-ROM that can help. Good ones often come free with magazines.

- Look out for TV series and magazine and newspaper articles on your subject.

Keep in touch

The Internet isn't just the world's biggest store of useful facts. You can also use it to communicate with friends, teachers, and even experts who might be able to help with your homework.

Ways of talking

There are loads of ways to send messages, chat, swap information, and ask for expert help on the Net. Here are the main ones:

- E-mail (or electronic mail) lets you send written messages, pictures, and files to anyone else who's on the Net.

- Forms are found on some websites. You fill them in with a message or question to get a reply.

- Newsgroups – sometimes called 'bulletin boards' – let you post up a message on-line. Anyone on the Net can read it and write a reply.

- Chat means having a conversation on-line. Instead of waiting ages for a reply, you and the person you're talking to get each other's messages instantly, so you can 'talk' in real time.

Using e-mail

Most Internet software comes with an e-mail program. When you first use it, you have to create an e-mail address for yourself so messages can get to you. (There are also some websites, such as HotMail, that can give you an e-mail address.) Here's a typical e-mail address:

This bit of the address shows who you are. It could be your name, a made-up name or just some numbers.

This symbol stands for 'at'. It appears in all e-mail addresses.

yourname@netcompany.com

This is the name of your ISP – the company that makes sure your e-mails get delivered.

You'll need to tell people your e-mail address if you want to get any mail!

Getting the message

Your Internet software will have a 'Get mail', 'Get new mail', or 'Get messages' button which you click on to collect your new messages. If you've got a message, it will appear on the screen. You click on it to open it up and read it. It will probably look a bit like this:

To:	This box shows the address the message is being sent to.
Subject:	This box holds a few words saying what the message is about.

This big box holds the text of the message. If there's a lot, you may have to scroll down to read it.

[Send] [New] [Reply] [Forward] [File It] [Delete]

New messages

To start a new e-mail message, click on 'New mail' or 'Create new mail'. Fill in the 'To' box with the e-mail address of the person you want to send a message to. Fill in the 'Subject' box with a short description. Then type your message in the main box, and click on the 'Send' or 'Send later' button. Most types of e-mail software will keep your message until the next time you connect and send it then. If you want to send the message straight away, click on 'Send now'.

If you can't see the right button, try the menus, too.

Replying

Replying to an e-mail is easier than replying to a letter. You don't need paper, an envelope, or a stamp. And you don't need to remember to go to the mail box – just click on the 'Reply' button! When you do this, your mail program will start a new e-mail message for you, with the 'To' and 'Subject' boxes filled in. All you have to do is type a message.

Attach a file

You can attach any type of file to an e-mail message, containing a picture, an essay, or whatever else you like. When you've written your message, click on the 'Attach' button. The software will then let you look through the files on your computer. You just select the one you want to attach, and click on 'OK'. When you send the e-mail, the attached file on the other person's computer.

LIBRARY
FRIDAY HARBOR, WA 98250

E-mail an expert

If you need help with a project or an answer to a question, why not consult an expert? Almost everybody working in universities and colleges has e-mail now. You can often find their e-mail addresses on the Web.

The Truth About Dinosaurs

by Professor Terry Dactyl

Professor Dactyl is head of the Fossil Research Unit at Dino University, New York.

Find your expert

First, find the right person to ask. Look at your school books: who wrote them? Or look in magazines and newspapers to see which experts get mentioned. To find the expert, use a search engine (see page 10) and search for their name or, if you know it, the place they work. Experts and universities usually have web pages with e-mail addresses on them. If you don't know who you want to ask, try searching for the subject you need help with. You should get some good university sites with the e-mail addresses of a few experts.

Will they mind?

Most of the people who work in universities and colleges will be happy to get e-mail messages from school children – as long as they don't get too many! If your whole class wants to ask the same thing, just send one message and give everyone a copy of the answer. And always be polite!

Keep trying

Remember, though, that experts won't always be able to reply. They might be too busy, they might be away on holiday, or they might just feel they can't answer your question properly. So give them a few days to get back to you, and if they don't, try someone else.

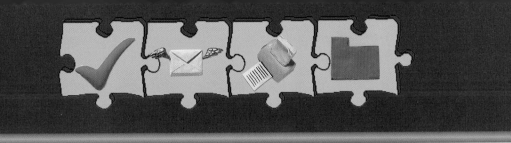

Ask the right questions

Experts will be more likely to reply to your e-mails if you follow some simple rules...

- Don't ask for too much. A short question that can be answered quickly is much more likely to get a reply.

- Don't ask questions that can easily be answered by a book or a website. The best thing about talking to an expert is that they can tell you interesting stuff that isn't in books, and things that have only just been discovered.

- Make sure your e-mail has a clear subject line that tells the expert exactly why you're writing to them. You don't want to confuse them!

Quicklinks
The **Internet @ction** website has links to places on the Web where you can ask for help from experts. You'll also find links to the Net's 'white pages' – web pages where you can find e-mail addresses.

Say who helped you

If you get a reply and you end up using it in your homework, remember to say where you got the information from:

According to Professor Terry Dactyl of Dino University, we do not know the color of dinosaur skin, but work in Australia shows that a 370-million-year-old armored fish was red. We may soon find dinosaur fossils which can reveal their color, too.

Politeness on the Net is called 'netiquette'.

To:	terry.dactyl@dino.edu
Subject:	Can you help a school student by answering a brief question?
Message:	Dear Professor Dactyl,

I am a grade 7 student and I'm doing a project on dinosaurs. I've read your book, The Truth Dinosaurs, but there's one thing I'm still trying to find out and I wonder if you could help. I'd really like to know if there's any new evidence to show what color dinosaurs really were. The deadline for my project is Friday, March 7. If you can help, I would be really grateful.

Thank you very much,

Helen Smith. |

Send	New	Reply	Forward	File It	Delete

World notice boards

As well as sending each other e-mail, experts all over the world use USENET. This is a collection of discussion groups, or 'newsgroups'. A newsgroup is just like a notice board – so try leaving a notice!

Newsgroup names

Each newsgroup has a name that looks something like this...

'sci' means science

'biotech' is short for biotechnology, the area of science that deals with biology and genes

sci.biotech.gmo

'gmo' stands for Genetically Modified Organisms

...so this newsgroup is about genetically modified plants and animals. If you wanted to find out about the new sorts of plants being grown in our fields, this group would be ideal.

Who runs this page? What does GM mean? How do I ask a question?

Reading the news

There are two ways to read newsgroups. The first way is through your e-mail program. Look for the 'News' button in the menu and follow the instructions to set up your newsreader. You'll need to type in the name of the newsgroup you want to connect to. Or you can read newsgroups through a Web browser, by visiting one of the USENET archive sites. This way, you can search all of the groups to find the useful ones, and you can do it without giving out your private e-mail address.

FAQs

Before you send a question to a newsgroup, check out the FAQs, or 'Frequently Asked Questions'. This is a list of all the questions people keep asking, along with their answers. It's good netiquette for new visitors (called 'newbies') to read the FAQs. If you don't, you could get told to stop bothering everyone!

Read the FAQs!

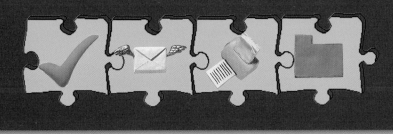

Ask away!

Posting a message to a newsgroup is like sending an e-mail, but instead of typing in someone's e-mail address, you type the name of the newsgroup.

To:	sci.biotech.gmo
Subject:	A question about GM carrots for my homework

Where in the world are genetically modified carrots being grown?

Send   New   Reply   Forward   Attach

Answers on a thread

Use a clear, recognizable subject line. Any replies to your question will have the same subject line, so you'll be able to spot them easily. Most 'News' software will organize the messages into a 'thread', or group, with similar subject lines, to make it even easier to find the replies to your question. Sometimes threads can grow very long, with lots of experts joining in and arguing about GM carrots, the color dinosaurs were, or any of millions of other topics. If it gets too complicated, just leave them to it!

Watch out!

Be careful: there are lots of people on the Net who want to sell you things, be rude or just annoy you. If you post a message to USENET then you may find yourself getting some spam. This doesn't mean that people will start sending you cans of meat! 'Spam' is unwanted e-mail, usually sent by people who are trying to sell you stuff. What do you do? Trash it!

Quicklinks

The **Internet @ction** website has a list of links to sites where you can read USENET. Go to: http://www.internetaction.net.

Chat

When you send an e-mail, your message sits there until the other person is ready to read it. But sometimes you want to talk there and then. That's what Internet Chat is for!

What phone?

Of course, you could just pick up the phone and dial the number of whoever you want to speak to. But people have been doing that for over 100 years and it's getting boring. It's a lot more fun to chat on your computer.

Cheap chat

It's also cheaper. If you connect to the Internet using a modem, then you pay a subscription to your ISP (unless it's free) and the cost of a local phone call (in some countries, this is free, too). It's the same wherever you go on the Net – and whoever you talk to. So you never have to pay long-distance phone calls, even if you're chatting halfway around the planet!

How to get chatting

Before you can chat you need the right program, like AOL's Instant Messenger™, or Yahoo! Communicator™. There might be a chat program with your Internet software. If not, it's easy to find one on the Web using a directory or search engine. Copy the program to your computer, then follow the instructions to connect to the chat service and register as a user. You will be asked to choose your own user nickname. Then you can run the chat program and look for people to talk to. It's best to use a nickname so that people you meet on the Web can't track you down in real life. Not everyone on the Web is friendly!

maxie

gameplayer

webhead

Video and voice

If you've got a microphone or a camera plugged into your computer, some chat programs will let you use the Internet like a phone or even a videophone. Read the program's own instructions to find out how.

Chat share

Chat is a great way to work together. If you and your friends are all on-line doing your homework, then you can tell each other about cool websites to visit, send pictures and examples to each other, and talk about the way you're doing your projects.

Chatting or cheating?

There's a thin line between working together and cheating, so make sure you're not just copying other people's ideas. Ask your teacher whether it's OK to work together on projects or homework before you get started, and always tell your teacher if you have done so.

Safe chat

The best plan is to get your friends to register at the same time as you, and then arrange to meet on-line. There are a lot of people on the Net and it's safer and simpler to chat to your friends. You can tell your chat program that you only want to talk to people you know.

Quicklinks

You'll find links to a lot of different chat programs on the **Internet @ction** website. It also gives you links to some helpful advice on how to chat on-line safely.

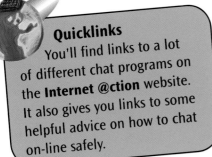

27

Be choosy

So you've found out how to search the Web, trade e-mails, ask experts for help, and swap info on-line. But don't stop thinking just because you're sitting in front of a computer. Use your brain along with your new research skills, and you'll get a lot more out of your time on-line.

Think books

Suppose it was the old days, and to find out something you had to look it up in a book. You wouldn't just go to the library, grab the nearest book from a shelf and look at any old page. You'd think about it first, find the right bit of the library, the right shelf, and the most useful-looking book. And you wouldn't give up if the first book you looked at didn't have anything useful in it.

Search the right place

The Net is the same as a reference book. It has different sections and different types of information, and some pages are much more useful than others. So every time you have a homework problem, think carefully about what kind of information will be most useful. Then choose the best way, or ways, to get help from the Net.

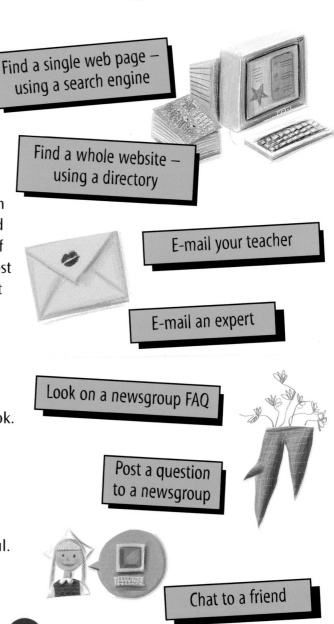

Find a single web page – using a search engine

Find a whole website – using a directory

E-mail your teacher

E-mail an expert

Look on a newsgroup FAQ

Post a question to a newsgroup

Chat to a friend

Homework helpers

Don't forget that some parts of the Web have been designed especially to help you with your homework. Look for TeacherNet, a collection of school websites. There are sites about every single subject you do at school, with facts and figures, hints and tips, and even places you can ask for expert help. Here, you should be able to find what you want for almost any project or assignment you've been set.

This homework is brilliant! Where did you find all these amazing facts?

A mouse helped me.

Pardon me?

I clicked on a great website!

Give a bot a shot

Lots of homework websites let you ask questions, either by sending in an e-mail or by filling in a form on a web page. Most of the questions are answered by real people, but sometimes you might meet a bot on-line. A bot (short for 'robot') is a computer program that can read what you type. It tries to find the answer to your question by searching through a big collection of information. Bots sometimes get stuck, but they can often help with simple questions and homework facts and figures.

What's the meaning of life?

Uhm...

Looking good

So you've got all your research done and collected the facts you need. But you can't just hand in a pile of bits of paper. You still need to get your homework reading well and looking good.

What have you got?

If you've been researching on the Net, you'll have a lot of bits and pieces to use. Well done! You might have...

- Pictures you've saved from websites.

- Selections of useful text from web pages.

- Useful e-mails or newsgroup messages from experts, teachers, or friends.

- Maybe you've even got sound or video clips stored as computer files.

Keep cool!

Remember that presentation isn't everything. Don't spend hours getting the type style just right or searching for the perfect picture. Your teacher will be more interested in how well you've done your research, and how well you understand what you've found, than in the color of ink you've chosen!

Putting a project together

Whether you're doing a big project, an essay, a story or a short report, you need to write it up just as you would normally. If you're using a word processor, you can copy pictures you've saved from the Web into your document, using the word processor's cut and paste function. Even if you're writing your homework out using a pen, you can still use the stuff you've collected from the Net. Copy down facts and figures and redraw pictures and diagrams – just like you would if you were using a library book.

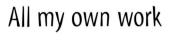

All my own work

Never copy long passages of text from the Web and pretend you've written them yourself! It's better to collect the facts you need, then use them to write your homework in your own words. Remember that if you use pictures copied from websites, you must say where you got them from. Put a note at the end of your project with the details and URLs of all the websites you got the material from, so your teachers can check it for themselves.

Quote... unquote

If you want to copy some text written by someone else, such as a poem, a quotation from an expert, or a description of something, put it inside quotation marks and say where you got it from, just like you would for a picture.

Getting it printed

If you've got your own printer then you'll be able to make your own printout, or 'hard copy', of your homework. If you don't have a printer of your own – or if it isn't a good one – then you may be able to use someone else's. You could always...

■ Save your work onto a floppy disk and print it out at a friend's house, or at school.

■ E-mail your work to a friend or a grown-up who can print it out for you. (If you're lucky, your teacher might be able to do this.)

■ Go to your local cybercafe or library and see if they'll let you print it out. (You might have to pay.)

Down-load cool pictures on-line!

Quicklinks
Need some ideas on writing up home-work or finding pictures? Go to the **Internet @ction** website for a list of sites that will help you make your homework the best.

If you spend a lot of time on-line, you'll soon see how useful websites are. They can contain words, pictures or sounds, and they are easy to change. So why not present your homework as a web page?

Ask first

Your teachers may not like you doing this – maybe they don't know how to use web pages yet. And if you're doing coursework for an exam, there might be rules you have to follow. So check first before you spend time and energy. (Of course, you could always build your own website anyway – just for fun!)

How pages are made

Web pages are written using a computer language called HTML (which is short for HyperText Mark-up Language). The HTML program for a web page is called source code. It contains instructions which tell your browser how the page should look on your screen. For example, the code for this page...

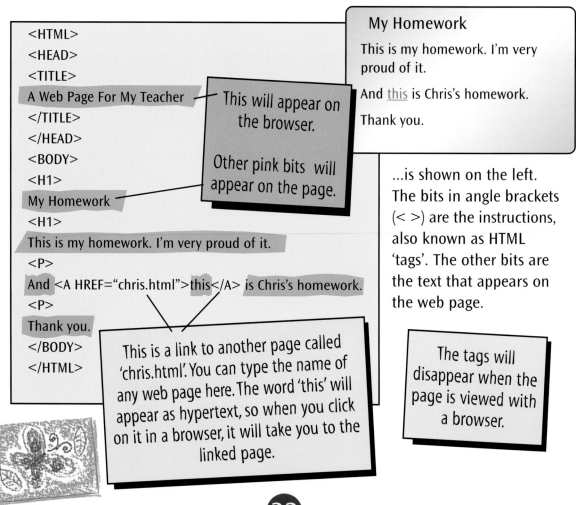

```
<HTML>
<HEAD>
<TITLE>
A Web Page For My Teacher
</TITLE>
</HEAD>
<BODY>
<H1>
My Homework
<H1>
This is my homework. I'm very proud of it.
<P>
And <A HREF="chris.html">this</A> is Chris's homework.
<P>
Thank you.
</BODY>
</HTML>
```

This will appear on the browser.

Other pink bits will appear on the page.

My Homework

This is my homework. I'm very proud of it.

And this is Chris's homework.

Thank you.

...is shown on the left. The bits in angle brackets (< >) are the instructions, also known as HTML 'tags'. The other bits are the text that appears on the web page.

This is a link to another page called 'chris.html'. You can type the name of any web page here. The word 'this' will appear as hypertext, so when you click on it in a browser, it will take you to the linked page.

The tags will disappear when the page is viewed with a browser.

Tag-tastic

There are lots of HTML tags – our sample page only uses a few (see pages 34 and 44 for more). But you could copy these tags to make your own basic page. Write the HTML in any word-processing program, and trade our bits of text for your own words. Call your first page 'index.html' – this is what most people call their home page. You should also save your page as a 'text-only' file so your browser can read it.

View the results

Then, to look at the web page as it should really appear, open it up using your browser. The browser reads the tags and uses them to lay out the page on the screen – but it keeps the tags themselves hidden.

> That's why you don't see HTML tags when you're surfing on the Web.

Quicklinks
The **Internet @ction** website has links to some good web editing programs which you can copy free from the Web.

Web editors

There are programs, called web editors, that will let you write your web pages without typing out all the HTML tags. Most of them work like word processors. You just type what you want, add pictures and other bits to the page, put in the links you want to other parts of the Web, and hit 'Save'. The editor does all the hard work, adding the tags and making sure the page looks right. Some web editors cost money, but you can get free ones on the Web.

Linking

The best thing about a web page is that it can have links to other pages – either to more of your stuff, if you've got a big project, or to someone else's stuff anywhere on the whole wide Web. To make a link, you just use a linking tag, like the one on the opposite page, and type in the URL of the place you want your site to link to.

Webs that work

There's a lot more to a website than some HTML and a few sentences. Most commercial websites cost a lot of money to build and have teams of professional programmers, designers, and writers working on them, but you can still do a good job just by yourself.

Get tagging

You can do a lot with your site, like adding pictures or sounds or even video. All you need are the right HTML tags. Some of the most important are:

<P> starts a new paragraph.

<IMG SRC="imagefile.gif">
will put a picture into your page. Just insert the file name of the picture you want to use. Keep the picture file in the same folder as your web page. It should be a GIF, JPEG or PNG file.

<HR> will draw a horizontal line across your page.

<BODY BGCOLOR="red" TEXT="blue">
gives you a red page with blue letters. You can use other colors instead.

<FONT FACE="Verdana" COLOR="red" size="+2">hello</FONT>
makes the word 'hello' red, a bit bigger and writes it in the Verdana font.

Are you streaming?

When you put a video or sound file on your website, the whole file has to be sent over the Internet before any of it shows. If you've got a big file this can take a while. If you 'stream' the file then it starts playing as soon as the first parts arrive. This is more complicated to do but a lot nicer for the people looking at your site. Some of the web tutorials you'll find on our website will show you how.

You can find lists of all the most useful HTML tags on the Web – use our site to find them!

Jazz it up

There's a lot more stuff you can include on your site, and a lot of it is there on the Internet just waiting for you to go and get it. You can...

- Put animated (moving) pictures and cartoons on your website.

- Have scrolling menus that make it easy for people to find their way around your site.

- Add feedback forms so visitors can tell you what they think.

- Add a page counter that shows how many people have visited your website.

- Make your website play a tune to entertain visitors.

- Choose from millions of colors, fonts, backgrounds, and fancy buttons, bars, and boxes to make your site look cool.

E-mail me?

Remember that there are a lot of people on the Web and you may not want all of them sending you e-mail – so think before you put your personal e-mail address on your website. Perhaps you could use a 'spare' address that's different from your main address. That way you can keep e-mail generated by your website separate from your personal letters.

> **Quicklinks**
> The **Internet @ction** website has links to lots of HTML tutorials with all the tags you'll ever need! You'll also find links to counters, graphics and other cool stuff. (And check out page 44 as well.)

Aa
Aa

So you've surfed the Web, chatted to the experts, sorted out your homework topic, and built yourself a website. But what's the use of doing a cool site if nobody can see it?

Ask them round

What you need now is a way to show your work to your family, your friends and, of course, your teacher. You can always show your brother or sister what you've done on your computer at home. And you can ask your friends round to have a look. But would you really want your least favorite teacher hanging around in your house? Of course not. So just keeping your stuff on your desktop computer is not an option.

Lug your laptop

If you're lucky enough to have a laptop computer, you could march around town showing your site to everyone who wants to see it. And you can take it into school for the teacher. But the number of people you can show off to is going to be limited. You need a way to get your stuff off your computer, and onto everyone else's.

Take a floppy

Your computer probably has a floppy disk drive. A floppy disk will hold around 1.44 megabytes of data – enough for a medium-sized website and some pictures. Some web-editing programs will let you copy a whole website onto a floppy (they call it 'publishing') so that all the tags, pictures and other bits work together just like a real on-line website. Once you've made a floppy, the person you give it to can use their web browser to open the 'index.html' file and look at your creation (check it all works properly before you hand over the disk).

Burn a CD, man

You can even put your site on a CD-ROM, if you've got a CD writer attached to your computer. It's like making a floppy but you've got a bit more space – 650 megabytes instead of 1.5! This means you can include video and audio stuff. But you'll need to get special writable CD blanks to do this – and they aren't cheap.

Get it on the Net

Of course, the best way to let people see your stuff is to put it onto a web server so it becomes part of the real World Wide Web. Then anyone with a Net connection and a browser can see it. That's about 200 million people around the world. A web server is a massive computer, and it would be very expensive to own one. The easiest thing to do is to store your web pages on someone else's web server. Most Internet Service Providers offer you free web space. Once you have copied your files onto their server then everyone can see them.

Hello! This is my website.

This is my pet. click here

This is my <u>fact file</u>.

Ask your ISP how to put your web pages on their server. They'll give you easy instructions to follow.

Don't forget your teacher!

However you publish your site, you'll want everyone to see how good your work is. But don't forget that your teacher comes first: make sure your homework is done before you start showing it off!

Quicklinks
On the **Internet @ction** website you'll find help with getting your website on-line. You can find places to publish your site for free and there are some useful tutorials, too.

As well as finding out facts and doing research, you can use the Web for learning tables or spellings, giving you ideas, or showing you the sort of work your teacher might be looking for.

Practise makes perfect

Sometimes you just need to learn something by heart. It could be dates from history, multiplication tables, or how to spell 'enthusiastic'. Memorizing stuff can be boring, but there are things on the Internet that can make it easier. You can get programs to help with spelling or times tables, or go to websites that will give you test questions (along with the answers).

e-help

For example, if you want help with learning your multiplication tables, there are lots of places that offer hints and tips. Type "multiplication tables" into a search engine, for example, and find some math help.

Getting good ideas

Another way to use the Net is to get ideas. If you've got a story to write, look at a newspaper or magazine site for inspiration. Or if you're looking at a certain period in history, try searching for stories about people who lived at that time to help you understand them better.

Art and science

If you're doing a science or technology project, you can find out about the scientists and inventors whose work you're looking at. And if you're doing art, there are thousands – probably millions – of paintings, drawings, and photos on the Net to get you thinking.

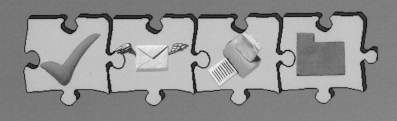

Check the competition

You can find websites where you can read other kids' work and see how yours compares. Stories, poems, art, photos, and – yes – even homework: there are millions of people out there publishing all their best work for the world to see. Lots of schools also have their own websites and these often have project work on them. You can find them by searching for 'school' in a web directory (see page 10).

Quicklinks
The **Internet @ction** website has lots of links to reference sites and school sites for you to check out. Go to: http://www.internetaction.net.

Don't just copy

When you're using the Internet for research or inspiration, be careful. There's a big difference between being inspired by something and copying it – and you should always make sure you do your own work. Taking someone else's work isn't fair to them, and it isn't fair to you either. You won't have learned much if you just cut and paste everything from someone else's website.

Searching sense

When you're searching the Web for sites, don't forget:

- Always look at more than one search engine or directory.

- Start with a wide search, and then narrow down: look for 'dinosaurs' first, then 'dinosaurs triassic'.

- Learn how to do advanced and Boolean searches (see page 12).

- Respect the boundaries your parents or teachers have put in place. Filter programs are there to stop you finding unsuitable things on the Net.

Hey! Get your hands off my work and write your own!

Work smarter

Once you've done your homework you will need to organize all your reference stuff in case you need to go back to it or need it another time. If you keep your work organized as you go along, you'll have much more time to do the things you really want to do!

Get organized

The Internet can help by showing you how to work smart. That means you can do your homework faster and better, and *that* means there's more time for the other things you want to do. There are lots of programs out there to help you make better use of your time.

> If you have an on-line calendar, you'll need a password to make sure no one else can read it.

Quicklinks
The **Internet @ction** website has links to loads of sites which will give you hints on homework for all sorts of subjects.

Keep a web calendar

Computers are good at keeping track of dates and times and places and things to do. But if you keep your calendar on your computer then you can only check it when you're sitting next to it. This is no use at all if you're at school – unless you've got your own laptop.

Remote access

But what if you keep your calendar on the Internet? You can check it by connecting to the Web at home, at school, at a friend's house, in a cybercafe or even in the library. Finding these sorts of on-line tools is easy – head for your favorite directory (see page 11) and type in 'calendar'. It's best to use a directory rather than a search engine, as you're looking for a website rather than a specific page of information. Follow the instructions to set up your own web reminder system.

To Do

Keeping track

If you make bookmarks (see page 14) of all the sites you like, you'll soon have dozens. Or even hundreds. It might be hard to find the one you want because there are so many. But if you organize them into folders and give them sensible names, life gets a lot easier.

science sites

art sites

web tips

castles topic

elephants topic

Get it sorted

Just select 'Bookmarks' or 'Favorites' from your browser's menu (different browsers call them different names, just to confuse you). Then choose 'Organize'. Your browser will let you create folders and give them names. Use the mouse to drag your bookmarks into the folders.

Ditch it

You can get rid of bookmarks, too. When you've finished a project, handed it in and had it marked and returned, you probably don't need to go back to the places you searched. So just delete the bookmarks you've finished with, or you'll have thousands by the time you leave school to go to college!

Vanishing act

Remember, websites can go away or change. Just because you bookmark a site, it doesn't mean the people who run it have to keep it going! So look through your bookmarks and check to make sure they're still current. Of course, if you've saved a copy of a web page on your own computer, you can always go back to it. If you decide to start saving stuff from the Web, set up a special folder for it. You could call it 'School', and then have subfolders for each project or piece of work you do.

Your favorite site could become a cobweb...

Well, it's all done. You've researched your facts, practiced your spelling, written your stories, and finished your drawings. Now you just need to get it to your teacher.

Into print

The easiest way to hand in your homework is just to print out what you've done and give it to your teacher. If you've got a good printer then this is easy. You might have to use a friend's printer, or one in your local cybercafe or even one at school (if you're lucky).

Onto disk

Your teacher may be happy for you to hand work in on a disk. Floppy disks are easiest, but you can make your own CD-ROMs if you've got the right equipment (see page 37). If you do this, you'll probably have to print a copy anyway to put in your work file. It's good to keep records of the work you've done and had marked.

Add your own art

It's sometimes best to do some of your work on a computer, using a word processor, and then print it out and draw the diagrams and pictures by hand. Most computer drawing programs are complicated to use, and you can often do a lot better yourself. So don't spend hours struggling with a mouse – just get the pens out.

In the mail

With some teachers, it might even be OK for you to send in homework by e-mail. This is the simplest way to get your work to your teacher, and the fastest. And you don't have to remember to pack it into your bag in the morning.

Will it work?

If you want to hand work in by e-mail, then check with your teachers first. You'll need to make sure they can read the files you send. Word processors and graphics programs all work in slightly different ways, so you might have to save your work in a special format before sending it. You should back up your work regularly and keep a printed copy too, for your work records and in case your computer breaks down.

On the Web

You can always create a small website (see page 32) and send your teacher the web address (or URL). Just check that it all works before you ask anyone to look at it! Other things to bear in mind:

- You will need to give the teacher a printout of your pages.

- The way a website looks depends on the sort of computer, browser, and even screen that someone has.

- If you want to remove your website you can do this by deleting the files from the web server you are using.

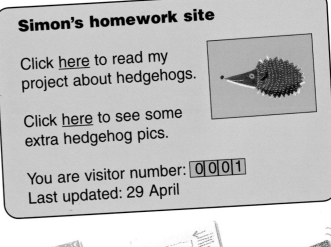

Simon's homework site

Click <u>here</u> to read my project about hedgehogs.

Click <u>here</u> to see some extra hedgehog pics.

You are visitor number: 0001
Last updated: 29 April

Extra website stuff

These two pages go into more detail about how to write web pages using HTML or HyperText Mark-up Language to create more advanced sites.

How HTML works

A web page is a computer file that's sent from a web server to your browser. It holds two types of information: the stuff you want people to see (the 'content'), and instructions telling the browser how to display it. The instructions are written in HTML, and are called tags. Most tags come in pairs. For example, these two tags...

<TITLE> My Website </TITLE>

...tell the browser to display whatever is in between them as a title. The text, 'My Website' is the bit that will end up as the title of the web page.

Open and close

The two tags that make up an instruction are slightly different. The closing tag has a slash (/) in it, but the opening tag doesn't. Here's a page of HTML. When looked at through a browser, this HTML appears as the web page shown opposite.

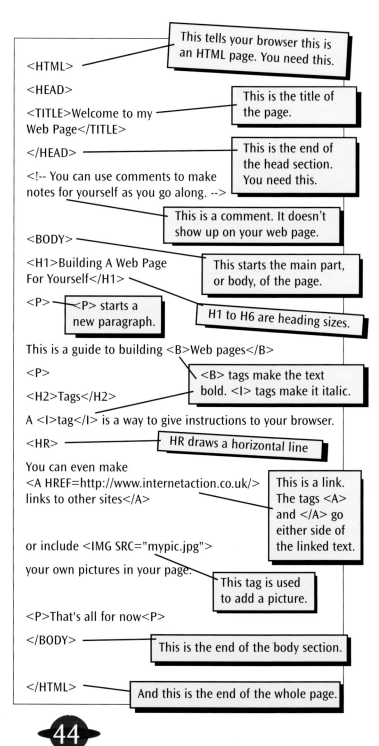

```
<HTML>
```
This tells your browser this is an HTML page. You need this.

```
<HEAD>
<TITLE>Welcome to my
Web Page</TITLE>
```
This is the title of the page.

```
</HEAD>
```
This is the end of the head section. You need this.

```
<!-- You can use comments to make
notes for yourself as you go along. -->
```
This is a comment. It doesn't show up on your web page.

```
<BODY>
```
This starts the main part, or body, of the page.

```
<H1>Building A Web Page
For Yourself</H1>
```

```
<P>
```
<P> starts a new paragraph.

H1 to H6 are heading sizes.

```
This is a guide to building <B>Web pages</B>
<P>
<H2>Tags</H2>
```
<B> tags make the text bold. <I> tags make it italic.

```
A <I>tag</I> is a way to give instructions to your browser.
<HR>
```
HR draws a horizontal line

```
You can even make
<A HREF=http://www.internetaction.co.uk/>
links to other sites</A>
```
This is a link. The tags <A> and </A> go either side of the linked text.

```
or include <IMG SRC="mypic.jpg">
your own pictures in your page.
```
This tag is used to add a picture.

```
<P>That's all for now<P>
</BODY>
```
This is the end of the body section.

```
</HTML>
```
And this is the end of the whole page.

44

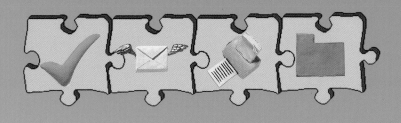

If you typed the page opposite into a file on your computer, then viewed it with a browser, it would look like this:

```
Welcome to my Web Page                                    _ □ ×
File   Edit   View   Favorites   Tools   Help
 ←        →        ⊗        ⬜       🏠        ⊗        ⬜        ⊘        ⬜ ▾
Back    Forward    Stop    Refresh   Home    Search   Favorites  History    Mail
Address │                                              ▾  ⟳Go  Links »
```

Building A Web Page For Yourself

This is a guide to building **Web Pages**.

Tags

A *tag* is a way to give instructions to your browser

—————————————————————————————————

You can even make links to other sites or include

your own pictures in your page.

That's all for now

```
🔲 Done                              🖳 My Computer
```

More tags

- The <BODY> tag can be used to change the color of your pages and the text in them. You do this by adding extra bits to the tag, like this:

  <BODY BGCOLOR="RED" TEXT="GREEN">

  ...although the colors may not always look very nice or be easy to read!

- Use <BR> if you want a line break without a space between the lines.

- Use <FONT> to change the appearance of the text on your page, like this:

  <FONT FACE="VERDANA" COLOR="BLUE" SIZE=3>

But remember that the browser that is showing your page may not have the same font, so your page might look a bit different with different browsers.

A note about colors

Colors on the Web are described in a complicated way because you have to tell your browser how much red, how much green and how much blue they contain. If you like you can use one of the sixteen standard color names instead:

AQUA
BLACK
BLUE
FUCHSIA
GRAY
GREEN
LIME
MAROON
NAVY
OLIVE
PURPLE
RED
SILVER
TEAL
WHITE
YELLOW

USEFUL WORDS

You may come across some unfamiliar terms in this book or in the websites you visit. Here are a few useful explanations.

.com
This appears at the end of 'commercial' websites and e-mail addresses.

.edu
This appears at the end of 'educational' websites and e-mail addresses in the United States.

.gov
This appears at the end of 'government' websites and e-mail addresses in the United States.

.net
This appears at the end of websites and e-mail addresses for 'network' organizations.

@
The 'at' symbol, which is used to separate the name from the computer-related bits of an e-mail address – as in bill@dial.pipex.com

advanced search
A clever search on the Web that narrows down the number of results you get.

animation
Moving pictures, popular on websites.

archive
A collection of computer files saved for people to use.

attachment
A computer file sent along with an e-mail message.

bookmark
See 'favorites'.

Boolean search
A type of advanced search.

bot
A computer program that can read what you type and reply to it. Used to provide information on the Web. Short for 'robot'.

browser
A computer program used to display Web pages.

bulletin board
A newsgroup – a way of posting messages on the Internet so that everyone else can read them.

button
An icon used on a Web page or elsewhere.

CD-ROM
A type of storage used for holding computer programs and information. CD-ROMs are plastic disks the same size as audio CDs, and can hold 650Mb each.

chat
A way of using the Internet to send messages between people who are on-line at the same time. What one person types can be read by everyone else.

cobweb
A website that has not been kept up-to-date.

cybercafe
A café with computers where people can use the Internet.

cyberspace
The 'space' you travel around when surfing on the Net. In fact, cyberspace is simply made up of all the linked computers in the world.

database
An organized collection of information.

directory
A website that has an organized list of links to other websites.

domain name
The name used by an organization or company on the Internet.

editor or **web editor**
A program used to create websites.

electronic mail
A way of sending messages over the Internet to other Internet users.

e-mail
The short name for electronic mail (see above).

e-mail address
The place you send electronic mail to for someone to read.

FAQs
'Frequently Asked Questions' – a list of common questions and their answers, often found on websites and newsgroups.

favorites
URLs that your browser knows you want to be able to visit easily. You can keep a list of favorites and add to them when you find a site you like.

folder
A collection of files on your computer.

format
The way information is stored in a computer file.

GIF
'Graphics Interchange Format' – a way of storing pictures on a computer.

graphics
Another word for pictures.

hard copy
Printed copies of the information held in computer files.

history
A record of the websites you have visited.

hit
A request for a web page or part of a web page. Every time a browser asks for a page from a server, it is a 'hit'.

home page
Either the first page your web browser displays when you start it, or the first page of a website you visit.

HTML
'HyperText Mark-up Language' – the computer language used to write web pages.

HyperText Mark-up Language
See HTML.

icon
A small picture used on a computer screen, usually to represent something.

Internet
A worldwide network of computers.

ISP
'Internet Service Provider' – the company that connects your computer to the Internet.

JPEG
A format for graphics files.

keyword
A word that you use to search in a website, directory, or search engine.

link
A connection between two web pages. On the Web, clicking on a link will take you to another page.

metasite
A website that has information on it about other websites.

modem
An electronic device that converts computer data into sounds that can be sent over ordinary telephone lines.

netiquette
The rules of good behavior that help everyone get along on the Internet.

network
A number of computers linked together to share information.

newsgroup
The usual name for an Internet bulletin board – a place where you can post messages which other Internet users can read.

off-line
Not currently connected to the Internet.

on-line
Connected to the Internet.

password
The word or phrase you need to type to get onto a computer or read information.

PNG
'Portable Network Graphics' – a file format for image files.

point and click
To move your mouse so that your pointer is over a button or link and click the mouse button to activate it.

save
To keep a copy of something, like the contents of a file or a website address.

search engine
A website that stores information about what is on other Web pages and lets you search it for different subjects.

software
Computer programs.

source code
The code that a computer program or web page is written in.

spam
Unwanted e-mail.

spider
A program that follows links between web pages, and sends information about the pages it finds back to a search engine or directory.

streaming
Sending information over the Internet so that it can be seen (or listened to if it's music) as it arrives, instead of having to send a whole file.

tag
A code used in HTML to tell a browser how to display a document.

thread
A discussion in a newsgroup or bulletin board about one particular topic.

URL
'Uniform Resource Locator' – the 'address' of a page on the Web.

usenet
All the newsgroups on the Net make up 'USENET' – short for 'users' network'.

videophone
A device with a camera and microphone in it that can be used to make phone calls.

web browser
A program that can request web pages from a web server and display them on screen.

web server
A program that stores web pages and other material, and sends them over the Internet when asked to by web browsers.

website
A collection of web pages on a web server, usually all about the same subject.

World Wide Web
A collection of information of all types stored on computers all over the Internet.

Yahooligans!
A Web directory just for children.

INDEX